SEX
and
RELIGIOUS
FUNDAMENTALISM

by

Angelyn Ray, MSW

<u>Sex and Religious Fundamentalism</u>

by Angelyn Ray, MSW

copyright © 1991, 2011 by the author

3rd edition, 2017

ISBN-13:

978-1463770341

ISBN-10:

1463770340

TABLE OF CONTENTS

This paper was first submitted in James Breedlove's Human Sexuality course at Portland State University, Graduate School of Social Work, Portland, Oregon, and made a part of his course curriculum.

It is even more relevant now than it was at its initial writing, when we consider the plethora of religious and political abuses as we make our way into the beginnings of the twenty-first century.

The topic of human sexuality is treated much like the thirteenth fairy, to borrow an allegory from the realm of fairy tales. The thirteenth fairy? We will get back to her, but first, a foray into academia...

Angelyn Ray

HOW DOES THE WESTERN CULTURAL FUNDAMENTALIST PATRIARCHAL/RELIGIOUS MILIEU AFFECT THE DEVELOPMENT OF HUMAN SEXUALITY?

Introduction

In this text we will focus on the various ways that our Judeo-Christian, patriarchal, fundamentalist heritage fosters the obsession-repression duality in our perception of our own human sexuality. The first five Life Cycle Stages posed by Erik Erikson will be utilized as an index of measurement in the child reared in the patriarchal/religious milieu that is at our roots - if not in our conscious minds, then in our collective unconscious, where there is a perceived deity on our coinage ("In God We Trust") and invoked in our flag salute ("one nation under God").

The ubiquitous presence of the fundamentalist, patriarchal belief system which has long been embraced as some citizens' idea of the "American dream" is still adhered to by a visible and vocal minority. It entails a belief in original sin (that all are born sinners), and in salvation from this sinful nature by an outside agent (Jesus Christ). Without a religious conversion on the part of the "sinner," and consequent submission to the "will of God," which for the believer includes affiliation with a church, agreement with its particular dogmas, and conformity to its tradition and ritual, the "sinner" remains condemned to eternal punishment.

Patriarchal fundamentalism as referenced herein is identified in a pamphlet by Nestor Perala of *Fundamentalists Anonymous*:

> "It is authoritarian, exclusivistic (they have the monopoly on truth and any other beliefs are false), legalistic (an abundance of rules and regulations), persecution complex (other churches, the media and society are against them), sanction-oriented (controlling the behavior of members by fear, guilt and

sanctions), hypocritical (presenting one face to the public and a different one to the members)."

Nestor Perala left a professional counseling practice to found a chapter of *Fundamentalists Anonymous* in Portland, Oregon, and to work exclusively with clients who struggle with leaving the religious system that stymied their development, yet remains at their roots. Why did he leave his practice? Because he found that so many of his clients' problems and areas of dysfunction stemmed directly or indirectly from religious upbringing or influence. (He himself was not so reared.)

In answer to the question, "What is the fundamentalist mindset?" Perala wrote:

> "It is a dysfunctional way of processing reality, characterized by massive denial and psychological dependency. It requires separatism, because separation from the world is the best shield against reality. The

mindset is a world of quick fixes, whether in marriage, family, health, sexuality or society. There is an inability to tolerate ambiguity and uncertainty in life, the inclination to paint everything in black and white, right and wrong, good and evil. This worldview allows no uncertainties, no unanswered questions and no loose ends.

"It is also obsessed with control - the strong urge to control people, to impose itself on others, and to be intolerant of differing viewpoints." (Nestor Perala's pamphlet.)

Trust vs. Mistrust

The first stage of ego development to be encountered by the human being is labeled by Freud the oral stage and by Erikson that of trust vs. mistrust. Since Erikson's stages are not to be grown out of and discarded like outgrown clothes, the handling of this stage, as all others, accompanies one through life, with the attribute of **_hope_** that is ideally the outcome.

In a child whose roots are patriarchal/fundamentalist, the beginning of discernment between the trustworthy and the untrustworthy is thwarted by a lifelong continuation of the infantile need to trust - to have faith without discernment. This occurs whether or not the infant has experienced with the mother the sameness, consistency, and continuity that mark a healthy achievement of basic trust. Erikson wrote:

> "All religions have in common the periodical childlike surrender to a Provider or providers who dispense earthly fortune as well as spiritual health; some demonstration of man's smallness by way of reduced posture and humble gesture; the admission in prayer and song of misdeeds, of misthoughts, and of evil intentions; fervent appeal for inner unification by divine guidance; and finally, the insight that individual trust must become a common faith, individual mistrust a commonly formulated evil, while the individual's restoration must become a sign of trustworthiness in the community." (Erikson, Erik, Childhood and Society, 1963, p. 250)

The fundamentalist parent, steeped in the threat of eternal damnation and the deep anxiety harbored thereby, yet loving the infant, seeks in fear to extract from the child conformity to church dogma. "Honor thy father and mother" (Exodus 20:12) and "Children, obey your parents" (Ephesians 6:1) are taught at the nipple. As a result of other common injunctions such as "Spare the rod and spoil the child," censure and punishment are meted out in order to secure conformity, and the child succumbs to an overwhelming sense of mistrust, for the world has been found to be unsafe, untrustworthy.

There follows also in the child, and undoubtedly with far greater damage, mistrust of the child's own feelings and capacity for discernment. This applies to all phases of life, including the sexual nature that is at the core of the human experience.

"The church is notorious for its obsession with and repression of sex. As one of my Catholic friends says, she was taught, 'Sex is dirty. Save it for your husband.' I believe that many of our most outspoken leaders of organized religion are themselves sexual addicts. They are so obsessed with sex that they make it impossible for church members to learn about healthy sexuality in church.... When an obsessive emphasis is put upon repressing sexuality, the result is often sexual addiction." (Schaef PhD, Anne Wilson, Escape From Intimacy, 1989, p. 39)

Erikson wrote that religions "organize the nuclear conflict of sense of trust versus sense of evil in the form of sin." He stated that organizations which may be formed to reinforce ego values at critical junctures of history typically outlive their historical ascendancy:

"Priesthoods...cultivated one or the other of the ego values, giving true comfort and providing true progress, but then for the sake of the survival of their own petty hierarchies learned to exploit the infantile anxieties which they at first alleviated." (Erikson, 1963, p. 278).

13

"Sexual addicts, especially those who commit incest, are often pillars of the church and the community. I can recall many painful moments at my intensives when women have uncovered deep excruciating memories of violent sexual experiences.... Her father was a professional man, a deacon in the church...I know now that this was not an isolated horrible incident." (Schaef, 1989, p. 31)

When the male head of the house, the model for the paternal introject, or when the mother, with whom the child first bonds in a nurturing natural symbiosis, operates out of the confused obsessive/repressive disposition toward his/her own and the child's sexuality, the foundation of basic trust vs. mistrust goes awry and the outcome of hope is displaced by pseudo-trust in overbearing, pimp-like authority figures and in a reaction formation to bonding (distancing and withdrawal), and by a certain hopelessness. Trust is turned against one's own well-being, and the ability to bond with other human beings is displaced by a tendency toward dominance or toward submission – bondage.

At the same time, the child is taught in church that "God is love" (I John 4:8), and that the commandment is "Thou shalt love thy neighbor as thyself." (Matthew 22:39)

> "What we have recognized as one of the techniques for fulfilling the pleasure principle has often been brought into connection with religion; this connection may lie in the remote regions where the distinction between the ego and objects or between objects themselves is neglected... readiness for a universal love of mankind and the world represents the highest standpoint which man can reach.... I should like to bring forward my two main objections to this view. A love that does not discriminate seems to me to forfeit a part of its own value, by doing an injustice to its object;

and secondly, not all men are worthy of love." (Freud, Sigmund, <u>The Future of an Illusion</u>, 1961, p. 102)

Autonomy vs. Shame and Doubt

The ***will*** emerges during the second stage of human development, which could be said to correspond to Freud's anal stage, where holding on and letting go, and such games as peek-a-boo, become the child's focal activities. This occurs at the toilet as well as other places.

> "The paradise of orality and its loss during the rages of the biting stage...may be the ontogenetic origin of that deep sense of badness which religion transforms into a conviction of primal sin on a universal scale. Prayer and atonement, therefore, must

renounce the all too avaricious
desire for 'the world' and must
demonstrate, in reduced posture
and in the inflection of urgent
appeal, a return to bodily smallness,
to technical helplessness, and to
voluntary suffering." (Erikson, 1963,
p. 147)

The anxiety of the fundamentalist
parent, based on a belief that the child's
eternal fate is in jeopardy, incites the
parent to undue coercive tactics.
Parental, hence "divine," mandate must
be obeyed. Children are taught
obedience to parents at the potty, and
normal grabbing and throwing activities
are seen as willful and sinful - acts to be
curbed by punishment and censure.

Older parents have been heard to
boast that their (now adult, disturbed)
offspring were toilet trained at eleven or
twelve months. Erikson viewed such an
environment as a breeding ground for
<u>doubt</u>.

What he said of the elimination process and toilet training is applicable as well to the spanking that is the norm in the patriarchal fundamentalist family. The thighs and buttocks being considered an erogenous zone, Erikson's observations concerning toilet training can be applied to the child's sense of his/her own sexuality when the "behind" is attacked and hurt by the parent:

> "This reverse area of the body, with its aggressive and libidinal focus in the sphincter and in the buttocks, cannot be seen by the child, and yet it can be dominated by the will of others. The 'behind' is the small being's dark continent, an area of the body which can be magically dominated and effectively invaded by those who would attack one's power of autonomy and who would designate as evil those products of the bowels which were felt to be all right when they were being passed. This basic sense of doubt in whatever one has left behind forms a substratum for later and more

verbal forms of compulsive doubting; this finds its adult expression in paranoic fears concerning hidden persecutors and secret persecutions threatening from behind." (Erikson, 1963, p. 253-254)

Depression with paranoid delusions, obsessive-compulsive disorders, paranoid schizophrenia and the like may result. In any case, for the fundamentalist, the <u>will</u> is subverted by the imposition of "God's will." Surrender to the will of God is the ultimate end of human potential to the patriarchal fundamentalist (to others, it can be surrender to a government that mandates moral codes through legislation - "In God We Trust" - a topic for another paper - or a school, a family).

The mythic model of sacrifice, celebrated every year on Good Friday (the crucifixion of Christ), with the sacrifice of the male and the abject sorrow of the female (his mother Mary and others), becomes a normalizing model. Easter (resurrection) follows Good Friday, but it is reserved for Christ; for the Christian, the resurrection comes only after death.

And in the virgin birth, celebrated every Christmas, either overtly or in myth and symbol, the sense of shame and sin is instilled in the child whose normal instincts would lead her/him into natural avenues for exploration of sexual urges. Christ was born without sin, of a virgin (implying fulfillment of human will and purpose without human copulation, without human sexuality)...

> "As other ego values (i.e., autonomy) become the nuclei of collective endeavors, older organizations may increasingly depend on a ruthless exploitation of infantile fears. A church may have to take refuge in a system of indoctrination intended to convince people of the inescapable reality of a particular kind of evil in order to be able to announce that it alone

possesses the key for the only door to salvation." (Erikson, 1963, p. 278)

Anne Wilson Schaef shows how this "ruthless exploitation of infantile fears" leads to entire civilizations which are run by the fears of their citizens, which, indeed, mandate codes embodying a morality that keeps the fears and the suppressed childhood impulses in nominal check. But we become what we resist. By resisting and attempting to repress the natural, primal instincts as embodied in our sexual natures, we become sexual predators and perverts, or otherwise sexually dysfunctional - at the effect of a human sexuality that is essential, powerful, undeniable, and virtually irrepressible. Or we become subscribers to the denial of our sexual natures, forever hiding from our own shadows:

> "Sexuality and spirituality are...fundamental aspects of the human organism. They are also areas of human existence over which the system seems to exert the

most control. I find this curious. What would happen if people (especially women, who are the most controlled) were in touch with their sexuality and living out of their true spiritual selves? Why has the organized spirituality of our society, the church, set up an obsession-repression dualism with respect to sex? How are spirituality and sexuality linked? We must also look at the way societal sexual obsession-addiction is used to control basic functions of the society such as mating and the formation of families. We must see the link between societal sexual addiction and incest and child molesting and must see that we cannot deal with these issues purely on a political level." (Schaef, 1989, pp. 43-44)

Ernest Jones called Christianity a sublimation of, and a defense against, Oedipal wishes, equating it with "certain mental phenomena of the anal stage." His militant atheism equates "religiosity and the established Churches with the acceptance of superstition." (Alexander, Eisenstein, Grotjahn, <u>Psychoanalytic Pioneers</u>, 1966, p. 115)

> "Primitive religions, the most primitive layer in all religions, and the religious layer in each individual, abound with efforts at atonement which try to make up for vague deeds against a maternal matrix and try to restore faith in the goodness of one's striving and in the kindness of the powers of the universe." (Erikson, 1963, p. 251)

Erikson explains superstition as borne out by his study of primitive peoples who developed a collective magic, treating perceived supernatural powers as if they were angry gods to be appeased by prayer and by self-torture on the part of the penitent consumer. Myths of punishment and divine retribution have abounded throughout history.

"Noah's flood" was sent to destroy the entire world because "the sons of

God saw the daughters of men that they were fair; and they took them wives of all which they chose." (Genesis 6:2). This, added to the violence among the peoples of the earth, was the biblical cause of the punitive, destroying flood.

The story of Adam and Eve is commonly depicted with the wily, deceiving serpent as the symbol of sex and the cause of humankind's eviction from paradise.

Even Freud's ill-advised "seduction theory," in which little girls are said to seduce their adult molesters and rapists, still crops up in the form of victim-blaming, for example, questioning a girl's or woman's attire rather than requiring accountability on the part of the rapist. Is this a throwback to the Garden of Eden, wherein Eve, the woman, is often seen as the deluded seductress while Adam, the man, merely acted upon his own natural impulses?

Initiative vs. Guilt

The third stage corresponds to Freud's "phallic" stage, wherein the outcome is the solution of the Oedipus complex. To Erikson it builds the ego strength of ***purpose***.

By now, only an unknowable deity could bridge the gap that has developed between the id and the superego; the task could not be undertaken by the child's own ego. Hence the child's ego is subordinated, relegated by religious authority to the nether regions where evil reigns and devils abide.

> "Hitschmann stated that the two supports of the religious person's belief in God are the memory image of the overrated father of his childhood, and his lasting need for protection. The ambivalence toward the father determines the

relation of mankind to its deities. Originally, the Devil and God were one and the same, a single figure containing diametrically opposed characteristics; the figure later was split into two. The repressed Oedipus complex, Hitschmann stated, sublimates itself in myths and religion." (Alexander et al, 1966, p. 165)

The sense of "sameness" between the inner and outer realities of the child - an inner wholesome wholeness - is missing. The alternative, in the form of an abstract and absent figure of God juxtaposed against an evil devil, is readily embraced. The natural bent to initiative and purpose comes to be invested in the church teachings and in an imposed concept of deity which is said to have the ability, incidentally, to purge away one's sins (by implication one's sexual nature as well).

Freud made reference to the "inhibited aim" of those whose development is affected by the premature experience of a lack of sameness between the inner and outer, the self and the object, and he connected this with religious upbringing. A look at society at large, with the barrage of commercialism that teases out sexual innuendo, movies that make sex explicit and often impersonal, bumper stickers like "Nurses do it with care," "Fishermen," etc., "do it" (followed by a variety of titillating quips), "Let an electrician check your shorts" - the confusion of sex with love, intimacy and day-to-day relationships - and with our explosion of sex abuse/sex crimes/sexual dysfunction - shows us that indeed the aim of something that is eminently powerful, innate and unconscious is inhibited.

An individual purpose in a child facing the development of initiative, who is reared in a fundamentalist environment, could only be made to conform to "divine," authoritarian mandate, the alternative being intolerable guilt due to an imputed alliance with the devil or other forms of purported evil.

To the one reared without a cognitive channeling of impulses into a recognized dogma - yet with the abounding code of fundamentalist, patriarchal morality that underlies the messages s/he receives at school, home, and elsewhere - there is no respite from the guilt, rather there is an ongoing affinity with the guilt.

> "Today, it is a well-understood tactic of mind manipulation that if an unknown and unresolvable guilt can be established among a group of people... that group can be controlled and subdued. As long as the target group accepts the possibility that the guilt might be true in some ways, it remains introverted and creatively unproductive. All its resources go into trying to resolve the 'guilt' that does not exist in the first place." (Swann, Ingo, Natural ESP, 1987, p. 88)

Industry vs. Inferiority

During the fourth stage, as in Freud's latency stage, the cognitive faculties are beginning to develop. In the fundamentalist child, the sexuality of the earlier stages has been successfully suppressed and the child is well on the road to sublimation, which may manifest in a religious conversion, wherein the survival of the ego is facilitated by an experience of transcendental quality which would enable the growing child to find the <u>hope</u> of ultimate approval and reward, the <u>will</u> (conformity with God's), and finally, the <u>purpose</u> needed for meaningful existence to continue - within the structure of the belief system.

Entering the stage of industry vs. inferiority, from which a sense of ***competence*** should emerge as an ego strength, a religious conversion would allow the child to compete meaningfully, but only within the narrow confines of the church, wherein obedience and conformity would enhance a sense of industry and diminish the sense of inferiority. Freud wrote:

> "Is it not true that the two main points in the program for the education of children today are retardation of sexual development and premature religious influence? Thus by the time the child's intellect awakens, the doctrines of religion have already become unassailable. But are you of the opinion that it is very conducive to the strengthening of the intellectual function that so important a field should be closed against it by the threat of hellfire?" (Freud, p. 48)

John Tettemer (Father Idlefonso), who was for a time next to the Pope, but who ultimately left the Church, wrote that he had to guard against a tendency of students in the Order to overuse the means by which they mortified their bodies.

"I was wary of permitting the use of too many extra devices with which the ascetics used to torture their bodies.... The saints in their earlier life were often carried away by an almost inhuman frenzy against their bodies." (Tettemer, John, I Was a Monk, 1974, p. 149)

We may not know the early individual experiences of such celibates; however, we do know how fundamentalist religious institutions frame sexuality for the child:

"With regard to sex, both the church and the school operate on the repression-obsession dualism and its corollary, the repression/acting-out dualism. I believe that obsession and repression go together. Those things we are obsessed with and we try to repress become obsessions. Those things that we try to repress usually find their way out (like water seeking a new path), and frequently we act out in ways that are confusing for ourselves and those around us....

"Aloysius, the priest...was caught in the net of the obsession-repression dualism. Despite his own confusion, he was teaching others about their spirituality and sexuality. I knew a nun who firmly believed that God was dependent upon her celibacy.... It is not just the Catholic arm of the church that is confused about sex and teaching the obsession-repression dualism..." (Schaef, 1989, pp. 39-40)

A Jehovah's Witness child in public school is obligated to refrain from birthday and holiday celebrations and from flag salutes, promoting the confusion, exclusion and sense of inferiority that compounds and complicates the repression of the sexual nature.

And who is to say that the ritual sexual abuses that occur under the banner of Satanism are not operating in a reaction formation to disappointed expectations of a beneficent "God"?

> "We are frequently told about our religious and political leaders' acting out.... Repression begets obsession, and obsession begets acting out." (Schaef, 1989, p. 40)

Identity vs. Role Confusion

The fifth stage might be said to correspond to Freud's genital stage, and ideally incorporates the hope, will, purpose, and competence of the preceding stages, allowing the child to enter into a sense of identity at the time when childhood merges into puberty.

The ego strength to be developed is ***fidelity***. To the patriarchal, fundamentalist child, fidelity to the church and to authoritarian mandate - to "God" - displaces fidelity to one's own identity and developing nature, both spiritual and sexual.

If identity means being at one with oneself, and fidelity is the resulting ego strength, one is reminded of Shakespeare, who wrote in Hamlet, "This above all, to thine own self be true, and it must follow, as the night the day, thou canst not then be false to any man." Role confusion, then, breeds infidelity, or an inability to conduct true, meaningful object relations and healthy, nurturing sexual relations.

> "Religion restricts this play of choice and adaptation... Its technique consists in depressing the value of life and distorting the picture of the real world in a delusional manner - which presupposes an intimidation of the intelligence." (Freud, 1961, p. 84)

> "As the healthy-minded enthusiast succeeds in ignoring evil's very existence, so the subject of melancholy is forced in spite of

himself to ignore that of all good whatever... So here we note the neurotic constitution... and if we are to touch the psychology of religion at all seriously, we must be willing to forget conventionalities, and dive below the smooth and lying official conversational surface." (James, William, The Varieties of Religious Experience, 1958, pp. 124-125)

The "subject of melancholy" is so entangled in unresolved disturbances generated in the preceding four stages that the achievement of the desired outcome of fidelity through identity is virtually unattainable. The defenseless developing child is open and vulnerable to the morass of role confusion.

Conclusion

According to Erik Erikson's first five *Life Cycle Stages*, the desired outcomes of hope, will, purpose, competence, and fidelity are thwarted, distorted, and perhaps even aborted in a child reared in a patriarchal fundamentalist milieu, perhaps to a lesser degree in children raised within a system that nominally adheres to a Judeo-Christian ethic.

Inevitably, then, society is rife with adults – parents, teachers, leaders, perverts and perpetrators – who generate yet more sexual obsession/repression.

In concert with each other, the two poles of obsession and repression play well into the exclusivism and judgmentalism found in religious fundamentalism.

The obsession plays into the perverse and predatory qualities of sexual dysfunction, while the repression plays into the secretiveness of the predatory practices and crimes, as well as into the censure of others who remain outside the fundamentalist fold, and who may or may not espouse and practice a healthier approach to human sexuality.

For of one thing we may be certain: The sexual nature in the human being is not going away in the foreseeable future, nor has it been absent at any time in known history. We can come to terms with it, invite it to the table and find a safe and comfortable rapport with the topic, or we can keep it at bay, where, like the thirteenth fairy, it will continue to cast its dark spells upon us.

The thirteenth fairy? Well, the story goes like this...

There was to be a royal wedding. In the bustle of all the preparations, it was discovered that the palace had twelve golden plates just the right size for fairies. But there were thirteen fairies in the kingdom.

Rather than be embarrassed over the lack of sufficient dining accoutrements, the decision was reached to invite only twelve of the fairies.

Then the question had to be answered: Who would be ignored when the invitations went out? The answer seemed simple enough: Why, the fairy who kept mostly to herself, the one who was least likely to cause a fuss.

It was this fairy, the one who had kept mostly to herself, the one who was considered least likely to cause a fuss – in short, it was the thirteenth fairy, the uninvited one, who, after the royal wedding, caused all the problems in the kingdom, who brought doom to the newlywed couple, and who cast spells of droughts and floods and all other sorts of disasters, which ultimately led to the ruination of the royal family.

There must have been another way, a way which would have included all the fairies.

If we invite the topic of our own nature, every bit of it, to the table – if we cease repressing it, thereby alleviating the obsession, perhaps many of the problems in our own realm can be mitigated, or at the least, better managed.

Will religion have to be abolished? Only the patriarchal, fundamentalist aspects, as defined on pages 7-9 of this booklet.

It would take three generations to turn it all around toward health and well-being:

In the first generation of such a turnaround, the adults are educated so that they can examine their own beliefs and discover, not if, but how, the obsession/repression dichotomy has affected their development. In turn, they modify their practice. This generation of adults educates the young in their care.

The second generation will consist of those educated young, now matured, who were exposed to healthy models as they explored and developed their own natures. Subsequently, they will not only teach but will naturally model those behaviors for the next generation. Hope, will, purpose, competence, and fidelity will blossom without impedance.

The new patterns are established in the third generation, which will have no direct experience of the dysfunction, and will only read of it in the history books as a caution against repetition.

Is it likely? Perhaps not. But it is possible.

Implications for Social Work practice and the effects on me while writing this paper

An observant Social Work practitioner or counselor can trace similar lineages of dysfunction in his or her client base. Furthermore, it behooves every Social Worker to educate him/herself about this insidious and pervasive influence, often overlooked because it is in fact so very insidious and pervasive.

The emerging scenario as I researched and put together the evidence was nothing quite short of appalling. Having been reared as a patriarchal fundamentalist, and having spent years disentangling myself therefrom, I knew my own experience and the observations made over a lifetime.

To learn, however, through my own research and study, that the picture is

41

not only as clear and stark as I had come to believe, but is soundly supported in both the older literature and the newer, caused a renewal of astonishment and revelation.

I entered the Social Work Graduate Program with a sense that the problem is even far more pervasive than I had supposed, and I proceed with the unsettling knowledge that there is very little education and training available to Social Workers and others in the counseling field that will prepare us to understand and alleviate the associated societal ills and mental illnesses.

It remains to each of us, whether lay or professional, to examine our own roots, and to adopt a mindset of ongoing self-awareness that will help to guide us as we navigate the values left to us by our forebears and espoused by our peers.

BIBLIOGRAPHY

Alexander, Eisenstein, Grotjahn, <u>Psychoanalytic Pioneers</u>, 1966, Basic Books, Inc., NY.

Berke, Joseph H., <u>The Tyranny of Malice</u>, 1988, Summit Books, Simon & Schuster, NY.

Erikson, Erik, <u>Childhood and Society</u>, 1963, W. W. Norton & Co., NY.

Freud, Sigmund, <u>The Future of an Illusion</u>, 1961, The Hogarth Press, Ltd., Toronto, Canada.

James, William, <u>The Varieties of Religious Experience</u>, 1958, The New American Library of World Literature, Inc., NY.

Monte, Christopher F., <u>Beneath the Mask</u>, 1980, Holt, Rinehart, and Winston, NY.

Perala, Nestor, <u>Some Questions and Answers About FUNDAMENTALISTS ANONYMOUS</u>, undated pamphlet distributed in 1990, Portland, Oregon.

Schaef, Ph.D., Anne Wilson, <u>Escape From Intimacy</u>, 1989, Harper and Row, San Francisco.

Shakespeare, William, <u>Hamlet</u>.

Swann, Ingo, <u>Natural ESP</u>, 1987, Bantam Books Inc., NY.

Tettemer, John (Father Idlefonso), <u>I Was a Monk</u>, 1951, Request Books, Wheaton, IL.

The Holy Bible, King James Version.

<u>Other books by the author</u>

EA101 – *We are Earth's Everlasting Arms in Embryo*

Fables by the Sea – *Award-Winning Tales from Land's End*

Ode to Earth in 9-11 Meter

Return of the Prodigal Genius

Sweet Influences – *Voices from the Void*

The Forest Dweller

The Gardener's Exile

The Nu I Ching

The Soul's Seasons

The Stickspeaker Collection

The World – Before, Now, To Come (*poetry)*

Why Not Blood Sacrifice – A Better Way

Wings of Comfort – *New Light on Old Scripture*

88 Keys to Well-Being

99 Passwords to Personal Power